the SHOT heard 'round the WORLD

by

Phil Bildner

illustrated by

C. F. Payne

Simon & Schuster Books for Young Readers
New York   London   Toronto   Sydney

SIMON & SCHUSTER BOOKS FOR YOUNG READERS • An imprint of Simon & Schuster Children's Publishing Division
1230 Avenue of the Americas, New York, New York 10020 • Text copyright © 2005 by Phil Bildner
Illustrations copyright © 2005 by C. F. Payne • All rights reserved, including the right of reproduction in whole
or in part in any form. • SIMON & SCHUSTER BOOKS FOR YOUNG READERS is a trademark of Simon & Schuster, Inc.
Book design by Mark Siegel • The text for this book is set in Golden Cockerel. • The illustrations for this
book are rendered in mixed media. • Manufactured in China • 10 9 8 7 6 5 4 3 2 1
CIP data for this book is available from the Library of Congress. • ISBN 0-689-86273-3

first edition

For Dad—P. B.
Thanks to baseball fans everywhere; especially my editor, Emily, who loves the Yankees;
and my agent, Jennifer, who loves the Cubbies and Twins. Let's go, Mets!

To my two sons, Trevor and Evan, for the joy and hope they give my life and our future—C. F. P.

If you lived in Brooklyn in 1951, your life revolved around the Brooklyn Dodgers.

Come summertime you bled Dodger blue. And it was in that summer of '51 that "Dem Bums"—what we lovingly called our Dodgers—caused their biggest stir of all.

Our Dodgers played their games at Ebbets Field, and since Dodger baseball was Brooklyn's religion, Ebbets Field was Brooklyn's cathedral.

With Pee Wee Reese and Jackie Robinson manning the middle, Gil Hodges anchoring first base and hitting home run after home run, and Campy Campanella flashin' signs for the likes of Don Newcombe, Carl Erskine, and Clem Labine, my Dodgers, yep, *my* Dodgers tore up baseball.

That summer my friends and I, livin' on Linden Boulevard on the outskirts of Flatbush, went to 'most every game, and when we didn't have Elsie tickets or couldn't sneak into the grandstands, we'd watch our heroes through the gap 'neath the metal gate in right center field.

I memorized every sign, sight, and sound: the *h* and the *e* in the Schaefer sign flashin' with each hit and error; Abe Stark's "Hit Sign, Win Suit" billboard 'neath the scoreboard; the sound of ol' Hilda Chester's famous cowbell; and the cacophony of the faithful Dodgers Sym-Phony Band.

Now, back in '51, things were a little diff'rent than they are today. The Yankees, Giants, and Dodgers all played in New York and, dependin' on where you lived, you pledged your heart and soul to one club and hated the other two with all your might.

I only had one friend who was a Yankee fan (but he didn't dare live in Flatbush). Like every Yankee fan, he was forever blabbin' 'bout Joe DiMaggio, Yogi Berra, Phil Rizzuto, Keller, Reynolds, Lopat, and *his* Bronx Bombers winnin' pennant after pennant.

I had two friends up near Coogan's Bluff who rooted for the Giants. The Giants played in the same league as us and with guys like Sal Maglie, Monte Irvin, Jansen, Mueller, and that kid Willie Mays, they won a few pennants of their own—I could always count on those two buds to remind me of that.

Yep, in that summer of '51, things sure were diff'rent 'cause '51 was the Dodgers' year. By the middle of August, we led the National League by thirteen and a half games. From Brighton to Bensonhurst to the docks of Red Hook to the streets of Bed-Stuy, all of Brooklyn knew that at long last the World Series banner was going to fly high and proud above our borough.

But then those Giants went on an unstoppable streak, a streak for the ages. At one point they rattled off sixteen wins in a row!

By the end of the season they pulled even with my Dodgers. There would have to be a playoff. Best of three to see who'd face the Yankees in the Series.

Yep, after a long, hot summer, the Dodgers, Giants, and Yankees were the only teams left standin' in all of baseball, and across the five boroughs every truck driver, transit cop, and trial judge was transfixed. Even the mayor officially declared it "Baseball Week in the World's Greatest City."

For the playoff opener hundreds of us crammed that gate in right-center, and we watched in horror as those Giants stole victory at Ebbets Field. Bobby Thomson, the Giant third baseman, hit the decisive blow, a home run off Ralph Branca.

Now the only way my Dodgers could win the pennant would be to take two from the Giants on their home turf, the Polo Grounds.

We sent Clem Labine to the hill for that second game, and we pranced 'round the living room as he pitched a game like no other. Shut out those Giants ten–nothing and, just like that, things were evened up.

It was down to one game.

One game.

Winner—the pennant, the Yanks, and the World Series.

Loser—wait till next year.

That afternoon of October the third was like none I'd seen before or none I've seen since. The entire borough of Brooklyn came to a halt. No matter where you looked, life was on hold for Dem Bums.

Up on Pitkin Avenue in Brownsville, the rabbis recited special hymns and prayers, and down at Lundy's in Sheepshead Bay, the fussy old ladies, forever complainin' about their flounder and snapper, put a fork in their whinin'.

At the Parade Grounds in Prospect Park—where the best of us baseballers played on fields #1 and #13—not a single kid tossed the rawhide, not a single kid shagged flies.

In the barbershops along Atlantic and Flatbush, no clippers clipped and no buzzers buzzed. Even the red-and-white-striped sidewalk barber poles stopped swirlin'!

At Coney Island—no line for the Wonder Wheel. No line for the Parachute Jump. Not even a line for the Cyclone. And if you hopped on down the boardwalk to Nathan's Famous Franks over on Surf Avenue, you wouldn't have had to wait there either. Doubt they were even makin' franks and fries that afternoon!

No egg creams creamed. No punchballs punched. No knishes knished. No trolleys trolleyed.

Everywhere you looked: From the Flatlands to Bay Ridge, on playgrounds, street corners, and front stoops, school kids like us huddled 'round radios listenin' to WMCA.

My Dodgers jumped ahead early thanks to a Jackie Robinson single, and Don Newcombe shut down those Giants all the way till the seventh. All they could muster 'gainst our ace was a lone run on a sac fly off the bat of that guy Bobby Thomson again.

In the eighth my Dodgers rallied big. Plated three more runners, and when Newcombe silenced those Giant bats in the bottom of the inning, we were dancin' in the streets. Even when we failed to score in the top of the ninth, we were callin' for the Bombers.

A three-run lead. Bottom of the ninth. Three outs to go.

Three measly outs.

But then . . .

Single.

Single.

And just like that the Giants were bringin' the tying run to the plate in the form of Mighty Monte Irvin.

We squeezed our Spaldeens and twirled our skate keys as our ace dug down deep and managed to get the Giant slugger to pop up meekly.

One gone.

But that was all Newcombe had left. The next batter lashed a run-scoring double.

4–2. Two on. One out.

Comin' 'round to the plate for the Giants . . . Bobby Thomson.
Pine tarrin' his bat in the on-deck circle . . . Willie Mays.

My Dodgers looked to the 'pen, and once again dialed up number thirteen, Ralph Branca, to face Bobby Thomson.

We huddled in and clutched hands as Branca took to the hill.

He fired a fastball.

"Strike one!"

He fired another fastball. . . .

CRACK!

"There's a long drive! It's gonna be, I believe . . . !"

Staring at the radio, we could *see* the ball sail toward . . .

Home run.

"The Giants win the pennant! The Giants win the pennant! The Giants win the pennant! The Giants win the pennant!"

Russ Hodges's radio call echoed through all of Brooklyn.

"Bobby Thomson hits into the lower deck of the left field stands! The Giants win the pennant! And they're going crazy! They're going crazy! Oh, ho!"

Giants, five. Dodgers, four.

"Fiction is dead," the papers cried the next day.

Think the unthinkable and believe the unbelievable because livin' proof now existed that the impossible did indeed occur.

In 1951 no Dodger pennant flag would unfurl. An entire borough numbed by the shot heard 'round the world.

Game over. Season over.

But you know what?
I still couldn't wait till next year.